*This book was purchased
with funds from a
generous donation by*

Dr. Kathryn W. Davis

MIKE LUPICA

CATHLEEN SMALL

Cavendish Square

New York

Published in 2015 by Cavendish Square Publishing, LLC
243 5th Avenue, Suite 136, New York, NY 10016

Website: cavendishsq.com

This publication represents the opinions and views of the author based on his or her personal experience, knowledge, and research. The information in this book serves as a general guide only. The author and publisher have used their best efforts in preparing this book and disclaim liability rising directly or indirectly from the use and application of this book.

CPSIA Compliance Information: Batch #WS14CSQ

All websites were available and accurate when this book was sent to press.

Library of Congress Cataloging-in-Publication Data

Small, Cathleen.
Mike Lupica / by Cathleen Small.
p. cm. — (Spotlight on children's authors)
Includes index.
ISBN 978-1-62712-849-0 (hardcover) ISBN 978-1-62712-850-6 (paperback) ISBN 978-1-62712-851-3 (ebook)
1. Authors, American — 20th century — Biography — Juvenile literature. 2. Journalists—United States — Biography — Juvenile literature. I. Small, Cathleen. II. Title.

PS3562.U59 S63 2015
813—d23

Editorial Director: Dean Miller
Editor: Andrew Coddington
Senior Copy Editor: Wendy A. Reynolds
Art Director: Jeffrey Talbot

Senior Designer: Amy Greenan
Production Manager: Jennifer Ryder-Talbot
Production Editor: David McNamara
Photo Research: J8 Media

Printed in the United States of America

CONTENTS

INTRODUCTION:
Sports+Writing+Kids=Fun

Nobody knows sports and kids like Mike Lupica does. When he was young, Mike played every sport he could, from baseball and basketball to cross-country and golf. When he got married and had four children, he became what he calls a "serial Little League coach," as well as a youth basketball and soccer coach.

What did Mike learn in those years of parenting his three sons and his daughter, and coaching sports teams? He learned about *kids*—how they talk, what they like, what they dream of, what they're scared of, and how they cope with their problems. He learned that kids, whether they're the best player or the kid who gets cut from the team for being too small, *love* sports. Any day playing sports is a good day if you try hard, do your best, and have fun while you play.

However, there's one thing Mike loves as much as sports, if not more: writing. As a kid, Mike loved to read and write, and as an adult he decided he wanted to turn that passion into a job. He was a sports writer and even a TV personality before finding his true passion in life: writing books for young readers.

If you're going to make one love of your life into your job, why not bring in the other loves of your life? Mike did just that, combining sports, writing, and kids into one amazing job. Today, in addition to working as a sportscaster, Mike writes sports adventure stories for young readers. He says it's so much fun that it doesn't even feel like work!

Mike is a frequent participant in the annual
Artists & Writers Celebrity Softball Game in
East Hampton, New York.

Chapter 1
THE SPORTS GEEK

When **Michael Thomas Lupica**, known as Mike, was growing up in the 1950s and 1960s, there was no cable television, no Internet, and no video games. While most families had a television set, there weren't as many programs to choose from as there are today. Kids didn't come home from school and sit down to watch TV alone; instead, their families might watch a show or two together after dinner.

What was a young boy to do with his spare time? If you were a kid like Mike Lupica, you either read or played sports. And, if you *were* Mike Lupica, you eventually turned your two favorite activities into a successful career as a famous sportswriter, talk-show host, and author.

Mike was born in Oneida, New York, on May 11, 1952. His father, Benedict, was a U.S. Army Air Force bombardier in Germany, Austria, and Italy during World War II. After the war, he worked at Griffiths Air Force Base in nearby Rome, New York. When Mike was twelve years old, his father took a job at Hanscom Field in northern Massachusetts. The family moved to Nashua, the second largest city in New Hampshire, located on the Massachusetts state line.

Winters in Nashua are long and snowy, but the warm, humid summers provided great opportunities to play sports outside. Mike liked playing different kinds of sports, including baseball, football, basketball, tennis, cross-country, and golf. He and his father went to many sporting events together, and while Mike enjoyed watching the games, playing was even better than watching! A love of sports runs in Mike's family. His sister, Susan, qualified for the 1984 Olympic Trials after finishing the Boston Marathon with an impressive time of under three hours on two different occasions (in 1982 and 1983). A marathon is 26.2 miles (42 kilometers), so finishing in less than three hours means that Susan ran at an average speed of almost nine miles (14.5 km) per hour!

BOMBS AWAY!

A bombardier is a crew member who is responsible for aiming the bombs to be dropped from an airplane. The word bombardier comes from the French word for "bomb thrower." Mike Lupica's father flew in a B-24 heavy bomber, also known as a "Liberator." During World War II, he flew in night missions over Austria, Germany, and Italy, after just nine short weeks of training.

The Baseball Hall of Fame
is located in Cooperstown,
New York.

When he was ten years old, Mike decided he wanted to have a career in sports. In 1962, his father took him to the Baseball Hall of Fame in Cooperstown, New York, and young Mike was spellbound by the memorabilia and history of the game. Two amazing sports figures were being inducted into the Hall of Fame that year. One was Brooklyn Dodgers second baseman Jackie Robinson who, in 1947, broke through the color barrier by being the first African-American player in Major League Baseball. The other was Cleveland Indians starting pitcher Bob Feller, a right-hander who made his major league debut at seventeen. Feller was the first pitcher to throw a fastball clocked at more than 100 miles (161 km) per hour.

BREAKING BARRIERS: JACKIE ROBINSON

Seeing Jackie Robinson inducted into the Baseball Hall of Fame would've been an unforgettable experience for any baseball fan. Jackie Robinson is one of the greatest examples of the inspiring nature of sports. Born in 1919, Jack Roosevelt Robinson, who went by "Jackie," was the first African American to play in the major leagues. He started at first base (later moving to second base) for the Brooklyn Dodgers in 1947. Despite widespread prejudice against blacks throughout the country at the time, and particularly within the baseball community, Jackie eventually led his team to six World Series and one championship over ten seasons.

Jackie's success helped pave the way for countless talented African-American baseball players who came after him. His breaking of the color barrier in Major League Baseball is considered a significant contribution to the Civil Rights Movement in America. In 2004, the Major League Baseball organization retired his uniform number, 42, across the entire league, forever commemorating his contribution.

In addition to his love of sports, Mike loved to read and write. He enjoyed reading mystery stories, such as the Hardy Boys series. He also liked the Rick Brant science-adventure stories. One of his favorite series was the Chip Hilton sports stories, a series of twenty-four sports novels written by Clair Bee, a college basketball coach and member of the Basketball Hall of Fame. The books were mostly written between 1948 and 1965, but they were reissued in the late 1990s and are still popular today. In fact, Mike says the Chip Hilton series inspired the most important themes in his own books: friendship, loyalty, and teamwork. By the time he was eleven, Mike was not only reading sports, adventure, and mystery books, he was also writing his own adventure stories.

When Mike entered Bishop Guertin High School, a private school in Nashua, he still wanted to have a career in sports. However, he wasn't a very big fourteen-year-old, so he knew a career as a professional athlete was unlikely. He did like to read and write, though, and he really enjoyed writing about the drama of sports, so he began to write for the school paper. In addition to the school paper, Mike wrote about high school sports for the *Nashua Telegraph*, a local paper that paid him $5 per story—not a bad salary back in the late 1960s!

After graduating from Bishop Guertin in 1970, Mike headed to Boston College in Chestnut Hill, Massachusetts. Mike decided to study English, since he had enjoyed writing while in high school and was an avid reader. Mike says he wanted to study English to expose himself to as much good writing as possible, because he had already decided he wanted to write for a living. By this point he had moved on from the *Hardy Boys* and was a big fan of Ernest Hemingway, whose simple writing style he admired.

During his freshman year in college, Mike wrote for Boston College's paper, *The Heights*. His writing caught the attention of Ernie Roberts, sports editor for the *Boston Globe*. Roberts asked him to write a feature story on Pam Lake, the best baton twirler at Boston College. Mike's story on Lake was on the front page of the *Boston Globe*—no small achievement for a college kid!

Mike began to work the night shift at the *Globe*, and after his junior year in college the paper offered him a job covering the area's professional football team, the New England Patriots. Mike would've had to travel with the team and miss his senior year of college, so he declined the opportunity. He decided that he only had one chance to be a senior in college, and he didn't want to miss it.

While at Boston College, Mike also wrote for the *Boston Phoenix,* a small weekly newspaper. The *Phoenix* was a well-regarded paper, and many of its writers and editors went on to become well-known in American journalism. Mike wrote for two other school papers as well. By the time he finished college, he had built an impressive portfolio of work.

Mike's hard work and perseverance paid off when he was hired by the *New York Post* to cover the New York Knicks after he graduated from Boston College—one of the most famous teams in the National Basketball Association. The following year, the

New York Daily News hired him as a sports columnist, making twenty-three-year-old Mike the youngest columnist ever hired for a New York newspaper. More than thirty-five years later, Mike still writes for the *Daily News*. He later branched out into radio and television before beginning his novel-writing career.

Although Mike is best known as a sportswriter, talk-show host, and author, he is first and foremost a husband and a father. Mike met Taylor McKelvy, daughter of a banker from Toledo, Ohio, in Bridgehampton, Long Island, when she was visiting her mother's house for the weekend. During the week, Taylor worked in New York City for the Perry Ellis fashion house. She continues to work in fashion while raising their children, most recently as owner of True Blue, a well-known boutique in New Canaan, Connecticut. In addition to her work in fashion, Taylor is a board member of the Connecticut Special Olympics. She has organized some of the organization's biggest fundraisers over the years.

Taylor and Mike married in Bridgehampton in 1986 and have four children together: three sons, now in their twenties, and a daughter, who is now a teenager. Despite all of the successes in his life, Mike says that being a parent is still the best thing that has ever happened to him.

After the birth of their children, Mike and Taylor moved to New Canaan. One of the wealthiest communities in the U.S., New Canaan is a small town about an hour's train ride from Manhattan. The family spends summers in the Hamptons, which

Lupica and his wife, Taylor, out on the town.

Mike loves for its beaches and its baseball on Saturday mornings in the park. He also enjoys participating in the Artists & Writers Celebrity Softball Game, held in East Hampton.

These days, Mike likes to play tennis and golf and listen to classic rock 'n roll, but his favorite thing to do is be with his kids. When they were younger, he coached his sons in Little League, youth basketball, and soccer, and his daughter is a champion horseback rider.

CHARITY ON THE BALL FIELD

The Artists & Writers Celebrity Softball Game is the longest-running charity event in the Hamptons. Those who participate have been gathering each summer for sixty-six years to compete in the softball game to raise money for various charities. The Hamptons are a group of small towns located on the tip of Long Island, New York. The towns make up an expensive resort area, and Mike and his family can count some well-known people among their "neighbors," including comedian Jerry Seinfeld, actress Renée Zellweger, radio shock-jock Howard Stern, golfer Tiger Woods, and rapper/producer P. Diddy.

In keeping with the famous residents of the Hamptons, the Artists & Writers Celebrity Softball Game draws many celebrities. Previous players and "Hall of Famers" from the game include actors Alec Baldwin and Chevy Chase, former president Bill Clinton, journalist and anchorman Peter Jennings, painter Jackson Pollock, singer/songwriter Paul Simon, Major League Baseball player and manager Yogi Berra, and many others.

Al Leiter (left) and Mike Lupica, both recipients of the Starlight Shining Star Award, at the Starlight Children's Foundation's 14th Annual Celebrity Sports Auction at Madison Square Garden.

Chapter 2
WRITING OR TALKING

As a student and writer at Boston College, young Mike Lupica had gained the attention of regional sports editors. When he graduated from college, Mike took a job with the *New York Post*, covering the NBA's New York Knicks. A year later, he joined the *Daily News* as the youngest columnist ever at a New York paper. Mike is now a syndicated columnist, and these days he writes four columns a week for the *Daily News*—two about sports and two about whatever he feels like talking about. One of his most popular sports columns is "Shooting from the Lip," which runs on Sundays in the *Daily News*, and he recently began a weekly political column called "Mondays with Mike."

As a columnist, Mike has a reputation for not being afraid to share sharp, pointed opinions about the worlds of professional sports and politics. Mike is particularly critical of the New York Yankees, as well as steroid users, Notre Dame's football team, former New York City mayor Rudy Giuliani, former president George W. Bush, and former vice president Dick Cheney. He has been a vocal opponent of the proposed West Side Stadium in

SYNDI-WHAT?

A syndicated columnist is one whose work is printed in several different publications, not just the paper the person writes for. Mike writes his "Shooting from the Lip" column for the Daily News, for example, but that's not the only publication it is printed in.

New York, as well as the Atlantic Yards project and Barclays Center in Brooklyn, and he is openly critical of the Yankee Stadium that opened in 2009. Although many people appreciate Mike's honesty, some disagree strongly with him. There are even websites dedicated to complaining about Mike's opinions and his work. This is to be expected when you're a well-known person in the dramatic field of professional sports—particularly in the New York area, where sports fans have very strong opinions about their teams. You just can't badmouth the Yankees without upsetting a few folks!

Although Mike's direct writing style may offend some, he has many supporters as well. He won the National Football Foundation's Jim Murray Award in 2003. The National Sportscasters and Sportswriters Association named him the 2010 New York

Sportswriter of the Year. And, in 2012, he won the prestigious Damon Runyon Award for journalism. The *Daily News* editor-in-chief, Colin Myler, described Mike as "one of the foremost journalists of his generation," and said that Mike has "what every columnist craves: a must-read factor." Clearly, a lot of *Daily News* readers agree that Mike has that "must-read" factor—he's been writing his very successful columns for more than thirty-five years!

Mike admits that he has the attention span of a hummingbird. Never content to do just one thing, he soon branched out and began writing for other publications, including a well-known column for *Esquire* magazine called "The Sporting Life," as well as articles for *Golf Digest*, *Men's Journal*, and *Sports Illustrated*. He began doing radio shows, and he has made regular appearances on *Imus in the Morning* for more than thirty years. He also ventured into the television world as a TV anchor for *The Sports Reporters* on ESPN, which he still works on as a recurring panelist. For a while, he hosted his own program, called *The Mike Lupica Show*, on ESPN2. He has been a guest on numerous TV shows, including the *Today* show, *Late Night with Conan O'Brien*, and the *Late Show with David Letterman*. He has also been a regular on the *CBS Morning News*, *Good Morning America*, and *The MacNeil-Lehrer Newshour*.

The world of television sounds glamorous and exciting, and Mike enjoys it, but he admits that writing is his first love—especially writing books for kids. But Mike didn't start his novelist career writing books for young readers. He wrote books for adults until he found out that writing for kids was even more fun!

Mike even gets out on the diamond himself now
and then, like when he threw out the first pitch for
the Detroit Tigers vs. Cleveland Indians game at
Comerica Park in Detroit in 2010.

Chapter 3
FROM COLUMNS TO CHAPTERS

Although these days Mike Lupica is well known as an author of books for young readers, he started his novelist career writing for adults.

According to Mike, his many years of work as a sports columnist prepared him to write novels. Just like books, good columns tell a story with a beginning, a middle, and an end. Columns and books both have to get and hold the reader's interest, and that is the point of the "game" for the writer—to keep the reader turning pages.

Mike's first book was an autobiography. In 1984, he co-authored *Reggie: The Autobiography* with future Major League Baseball Hall of Famer Reggie Jackson, an outfielder with the California Angels at the time. Three years later, he co-authored *Parcells: Autobiography of the Biggest Giant of Them All* with New York Giants coach Bill Parcells, a future National Football League Hall of Famer who led the Giants to two Super Bowl wins in the 1980s and 1990s.

In between co-authoring the two autobiographies, Mike tried his hand at fiction writing. Interestingly, his first solo novel,

"PLAY" WRITING

You've probably heard of a screenplay, or the script for a big-screen movie, but you may not have heard of a teleplay. A teleplay is simply a script written for television. A third type of "play" is a stage play, which is a script written to be performed on a live theater stage.

Dead Air, was not about sports. Instead, like the *Hardy Boys* books Mike loved as a kid, it was a mystery—and a successful one at that! The book earned Mike a nomination for the Edgar Allen Poe Award for Best First Mystery and was turned into a CBS television movie called *Money, Power, Murder*. Mike further expanded his writing portfolio by writing the teleplay for the movie.

Next up for Mike in 1998 was a joint effort with William Goldman, entitled *Wait Till Next Year: The Story of a Season When What Should've Happened Didn't, and What Could've Gone Wrong Did*. It chronicled the lackluster 1987 professional sports season in New York City, which had been a colossal disappointment for the city's sports fans. The defending Major League Baseball champion Mets missed the playoffs, as did the National Football League's

Giants. The Yankees finished fourth in their MLB division, and the NFL's Jets finished fifth in theirs. For a diehard New York sports fan like Mike, the season was a bitter disappointment. However, it did provide him with some good material to write the book!

That same year, Mike published *Shooting from the Lip*, a collection of his top "Shooting from the Lip" sports columns, as well as a follow-up book to *Dead Air*. *Extra Credits*, Mike's second novel, featured the same main character as *Dead Air*, solving a new mystery.

Mike's third novel, *Limited Partner*, published in 1990, was another mystery featuring the same protagonist. This time, Mike introduced some elements of the sports fiction he would later embrace. While the plot does not have much to do with sports, a couple of the characters are former or current New York Mets baseball players.

After the publication of *Limited Partner*, Mike took a break from writing books for a while, and concentrated instead on his work for newspapers and magazines. It would be five years before his next novel, *Jump*, a mystery set in the world of professional basketball, was published. The following year, Mike returned to nonfiction with the publication of *Mad as Hell: How Sports Got Away from the Fans—and How We Get It Back*, which looked at the world of sports (and fans).

Mike followed *Mad as Hell* in 1999 with *Summer of '98: When Homers Flew, Records Fell, and Baseball Reclaimed America*. With *Summer of '98*, Mike started introducing kids into his narratives by writing about his sons' experience during the incredible baseball season of 1998, when the New York Yankees won their twenty-fourth World Series. Mark McGwire and Sammy Sosa were locked in a battle for the single-season home-run record. As if that wasn't exciting enough, the summer of 1998 saw not one but two more milestones as well. David Wells pitched a perfect game—the fifteenth perfect game in the history of Major League Baseball, and the first regular-season perfect game by a Yankee pitcher. Meanwhile, Cal Ripken, Jr. of the Baltimore Orioles ended his seventeen-year streak of consecutive games played: 2,632 games in all. Previously, the record had been held for fifty-six years by New York Yankees first baseman Lou Gehrig, who played 2,130 consecutive games from 1923 to 1939—a number long considered unbreakable.

Five years after his last fiction venture, *Jump*, Mike published *Bump and Run* in 2000. With this story of a seedy Las Vegas casino go-to guy who inherits an NFL team and tries to shepherd them to the Super Bowl, Mike left the world of mysteries behind—at least temporarily—and began to move more into writing fiction books about sports.

He continued this writing trend with his next novels for adults— 2001's *Full Court Press*, a fictional story about the first woman signed to the NBA, 2002's baseball story *Wild Pitch*, and 2003's follow-up to *Bump and Run*, titled *Red Zone*. In 2004, Mike went back to combining his two favorite genres—mystery and sports— with *Too Far*, a basketball mystery/thriller that, at this point, is the last book for adults Mike has written.

McGWIRE VERSUS SOSA: BATTLE FOR THE HOME-RUN RECORD

In 1998, America was captivated by a race to see who could break Roger Maris' long-held record of hitting sixty-one home runs in a single season, which Maris set in 1961. The two contenders were St. Louis Cardinals first baseman Mark McGwire and Chicago Cubs outfielder Sammy Sosa. In the end, both men broke Maris' record, although Mark McGwire earned the crown with seventy home runs to Sosa's sixty-six. In an interesting twist, McGwire officially broke the record in a September 8, 1998 home game against the Cubs, with Sosa in right field and Maris' family in the stands. The home run chase was widely considered to have restored Major League Baseball to fans' good graces after the 1994 labor dispute that cancelled that year's World Series.

A turning point in Mike's career came in 2004: He wrote his first book for kids. From that point forward, Mike has focused his novel-writing energy on creating books for young readers.

A post-game celebration like this one inspired
Mike Lupica to write his first book for young readers.

Chapter 4
A RETURN TO CHILDHOOD

Mike Lupica is a sort of Renaissance man in the world of writing, capable of writing many different genres well. His work spans many areas, from mysteries to sports writing, for audiences both young and old. He has written successful newspaper columns for more than thirty-five years. He has written articles for some of the biggest magazines in the industry. He has written the teleplay for a TV adaption of one of his novels. On top of all of that, he has written autobiographies, nonfiction books, fiction novels for adults, and fiction books for young readers.

These days, Mike's primary audience for his books is kids from age eight through early teens. Young readers are drawn to his action-filled stories about kids they can relate to—kids just like them. According to Mike's readers, they like his books because the kids in them sound like real kids—as they should! Although Mike doesn't usually model his characters after one particular person, he gets the ideas for his characters' personalities and dialogue by listening to his own kids and the children he has coached in sports over the years. When driving his kids to and from their games, and while he coached their Little League teams, Mike spent years listening to what the kids talked about. This gave him a lot of material when he started writing books for young people.

Mike has become a very successful author of books for young readers. There's one person in particular he can thank for starting it all: his middle son, who indirectly provided the inspiration for him to start writing for kids.

When Mike's son was in seventh grade, he was cut from the basketball team for being too small. Mike understood as an athlete himself that the choice had to be made for the good of the team. Still, he felt badly for kids like his son who wanted to play but couldn't. As Mike said, "It was the first time I had seen sports break my son's heart."

Mike took all the kids who were cut from the team and started a new team called the New Canaan Rebels. He hired a coach, bought uniforms, and scheduled games. Although the team started out losing to everyone, they improved in skill as the basketball season progressed. Mike says, "These kids never lost their love of the game. And eventually, they got good." Mike encouraged the players by telling them, "We're not in any league here… But every time you go out, you're playing for the championship of every kid who ever got told by an adult he wasn't good enough."

On the last day of the season, the New Canaan Rebels played a tough team that had previously beaten them badly. Despite what people may have predicted, the game was close until a free throw by the Rebels in the final three seconds of play won them the game.

The players went wild, celebrating as if they had just won the World Series, and Mike was ecstatic. Even more than being thrilled, however, he was inspired.

Mike couldn't get the New Canaan Rebels' victory and excitement out of his mind, and he talked to his agent about it. She joined in his enthusiasm and suggested he write a book about it. And so, Mike wrote his first novel for young readers, *Travel Team*. The hero of *Travel Team*, Danny Walker, is a twelve-year-old who is cut from his local traveling basketball team for being too small. Danny's father pulls together the kids who were cut from the team or who didn't try out. Together they form a new team of players that know the key to playing well is playing with heart. The book ended up being a *New York Times* #1 bestseller, launching Mike's new career as one of the country's best-selling authors for young readers.

Mike's second book for young people, *Heat*, also reached the top of the *New York Times* Best Seller List. With *Heat*, Mike moved from basketball to baseball, telling the story of Michael Arroyo, a young Cuban immigrant with an amazing pitching arm who spends much of his time hiding from bill collectors and the foster care system. Baseball is Michael's life and passion, and he aspires to play in the Little League World Series. But a rival accuses Michael of being older than the league's age limit, and parentless Michael has no way to prove that he's not.

Part of what makes Mike's books so appealing is that they not only focus on sports and contain a good amount of humor, they also deal with real-life situations and problems that kids encounter. As Mike

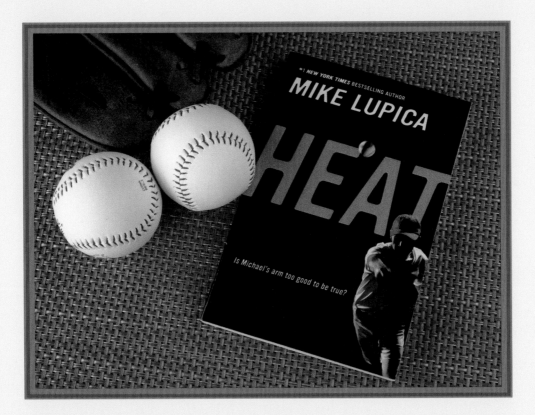

says, it's never smooth sailing for the characters in his books; they're going to face some problems. In *Heat*, for example, main character Michael is an orphan who is trying to avoid being sent to foster care.

In his next book, *Miracle on 49th Street*, Mike tackled the topic of difficult father-daughter relationships. The main characters are twelve-year-old Molly Parker and her father, Josh, a professional basketball player. In the novel, Josh is not even aware Molly exists until she shows up in his life after her mother's death. Josh is used to focusing on only basketball and himself, and he and Molly face some tough challenges as they get to know each other.

Around the time *Miracle on 49th Street* was published, a

book publishing company called Scholastic asked Mike to create a new series for slightly younger readers. In response, Mike started writing the Comeback Kids series, which became a great success for Scholastic. The first book in the Comeback Kids series, *Hot Hand*, deals with young Billy Raynor, the best shooter in his basketball league, and the challenges he faces with his fragmented family—his newly separated parents, his absentee mother, and his increasingly distant brother. The second book in the series, *Two-Minute Drill*, follows unlikely friends Chris Conlan, sixth-grade star quarterback, and Scott Parry, the brainy new kid.

Mike returned to baseball with *Safe at Home*, in which the main character, Nick, is in the foster system and struggling with school. The talented twelve-year-old also plays catcher for the school's varsity baseball team, and in trying to prove himself to his team and his foster parents, Nick learns a lot about himself.

Mike's next book outside of the Comeback Kids series, *Summer Ball*, is the sequel to *Travel Team*. Danny Walker, the hero of *Travel Team*, is headed to basketball camp after leading the travel team to the national championship. But competition at the camp is a whole lot more fierce than at home, and Danny questions whether he's really good enough at basketball to compete.

Each of these books point to a clear theme: The heroes in Mike's books aren't the kids who have easy lives where everything goes right for them. They're all facing struggles, and sports help them cope with the difficult parts of their lives. For these kids, sports are both therapy and the chance to succeed.

By this time, Mike was writing a lot of books. *Summer Ball* was quickly followed up by *The Big Field*, a baseball novel. In it, the main character, Hutch, learns a valuable lesson about being a good teammate when a new player is given Hutch's long-held shortstop position on the baseball team.

Being a good teammate is an important lesson to Mike, who says, "It's as important to be a good friend and a good teammate as a good player." Sportsmanship and being a good teammate are common themes in Mike's books. One of his latest books, *True Legend*, is the story of a young basketball star who develops an unhealthy ego and has to be reminded of the idea of being a good teammate.

Teammates and friendship are especially strong themes in the Comeback Kids series. The books in the series—*Hot Hand*, *Two-Minute Drill, Safe at Home, Long Shot*, and *Shoot-Out*—all deal with conflicts between teammates or friends, and how the heroes of the books deal with these conflicts on the court or the field. *Shoot-Out*, the most recent book in the Comeback Kids series, takes Mike's writing in a slightly new direction—the story is about a soccer player, one of the few sports Mike hasn't played. Compared to basketball, football, and baseball, soccer is a relatively new sport in America. It has been popular for many years in other countries, but in general Americans have only relatively recently become fans of the sport.

Friendship is at the heart of *Million-Dollar Throw,* too. In that book, thirteen-year-old Nate Brodie is nicknamed "Brady" because of his admiration for New England Patriots quarterback

Tom Brady and for his own passing ability. Brady hopes to win a million dollars by throwing a pass through a target at a Patriots game. Facing pressure from family problems and trouble with his passing arm, he remains inspired by his best friend, Abby, who is going blind and losing her ability to paint but never complains. His friendship with Abby drives Brady to continue his quest for the million-dollar throw.

COACH LUPICA

Mike believes that sports are valuable for every kid—even those kids who aren't the best players and who don't take home the trophies. Not everyone needs to be a champion to appreciate sports, he says. "It's about teamwork, it's about friendship, and it's about love of the game." Even if you weren't the trophy winner, if you can come away from a game saying that you tried your best, played your hardest, and had fun, then you had a good day in sports.

When Mike was coaching sports, he taught his players to see the value in each game they played. He told them to think of each game as a valuable coin. Every parent and every fan in the stands, he told his players, would give anything to be out there on the field or the court, playing the game. Getting the chance to play is valuable, and Mike reminded his players of that every single game day. And, as he was quick to remind his players, "This ain't a job; this is playing ball with your buddies, and if you can't do that with a smile on your face, we're all wasting our time."

Lupica and actor Kevin James read Long Shot at the NBA Store in New York City.

In addition to sportsmanship, teammates, and friendship, father/son and father/daughter relationships are at the heart of many of Mike's books. Fathers are important figures in *Hot Hand*, *Long Shot*, *Safe at Home*, *Travel Team*, *Miracle on 49th Street*, *The Big Field*, *Million-Dollar Throw*, and *The Underdogs*. And fourteen-year-old Brian's relationship with his absent father is at the center of *The Batboy*, along with Brian's growing friendship with a Major League Baseball player trying to make a comeback.

Although Mike doesn't typically base his characters on any specific person, he does draw inspiration from people, such as family members, kids he has coached, and occasionally even sports celebrities. In his novel *QB1*, Mike again looks at fathers and sons, but this time his characters are based on a real-life football family: quarterback Archie Manning and his two Super Bowl-winning sons, Peyton and Eli. In *QB1*, fourteen-year-old Jake Cullen is a quarterback for his high-school football team, but he has a lot to live up to. His older brother, Wyatt, is a champion high school quarterback, and their father, Troy, is a famous former NFL quarterback. Though socially awkward at times, Jake is always a good teammate, but he has to learn to be a winner and how to live with his family's celebrity.

In *True Legend*, the main character is also inspired by real-life sports heroes. The main character is basketball star Drew Robinson, who was modeled on a combination of Miami Heat forward LeBron James and Los Angeles Clippers guard Chris Paul.

In 2010, Mike made an abrupt turn away from writing about sports. His novel *Hero* sticks to one of Mike's favorite themes—a father and son—but instead of a sports story, *Hero* is an adventure story about a reluctant fourteen-year-old superhero named Zach. Zach's father, a government agent who solves international crises at the president's request, is killed while on a covert mission. Zach steps in to find out who killed his father, and why. As he investigates his father's death, Zach becomes aware of his father's superpowers—and his own.

Mike returned to writing about sports in 2011, when he published *The Underdogs*, which follows young football hero Will Tyler as he attempts to rally his depressed town with his love of the game.

In 2012, Mike launched his latest series, Game Changers, which is aimed at readers in third through fifth grades. Like most of his other books for young readers, the Game Changers books are

Sports fans at the Tigers vs. Indians game at Detroit's Comerica Park in 2010 got a treat— a chance to have Mike sign their books.

New York Times bestsellers. The first book, called *Game Changers*, introduces readers to football teammates Ben McBain and Shawn O'Brien. In the second book, *Play Makers*, Ben and Shawn make the switch from football to playing basketball for their school. In the third book, *Heavy Hitters,* Ben and his friends have a new teammate on their baseball team—a struggling kid named Justin. As with many of Mike's books, being a good teammate is at the heart of these stories.

FROM SPORTS TO SUPERHEROES

Why the change from sports stories to superheroes in *Hero*? Mike says he was inspired by a question from his editor: Would you rather be invisible or be able to fly? By asking many of his own family and friends this same question, he learned that many of them had very strong opinions about which superpower they would like to have. This inspired him to create a hero who has both powers. Mike enjoyed reading comic books while he was growing up, so it felt very natural for him to write *Hero*. (For the record, Mike says if he had to choose, he'd want to be able to fly!)

Let's play ball! Mike poses before throwing out the first pitch at the Tigers vs. Indians game in Detroit in 2010.

Chapter 5
WHAT'S NEXT FOR MIKE?

Mike Lupica is nothing if not a prolific writer. While keeping up several newspaper columns, writing for magazines, and appearing on radio and television shows, he cranks out bestseller after bestseller at an astonishing rate. Which of these jobs does Mike consider his "day job?" He says he doesn't like to distinguish between them. His wife, Taylor, however, has an opinion on the matter. Given the amount of time her husband spends on his work, she thinks they're all "day jobs!"

One thing is for certain, though: Mike is passionate about writing books for young readers. He wants those books on the shelf to be the thing he's remembered most for—even more than the columns he has written and the TV shows he's appeared on. When asked about his career, Mike says, "Let me tell you something about television: If I can be on television, anybody can be on television. I love writing these stories. I love making these kids come to life."

Mike comments that a great writer once said, "The fun of writing is finding out things you didn't know you knew." When he writes books, it is a journey of discovery for Mike.

He is also constantly amazed and inspired by how much kids still want to read. Mike notes that with all the things kids could be doing today—surfing the Internet, watching TV, texting each other—they still love a good story. Kids show up to see Mike talk with their favorite books clutched in their hands, and they tell him how much reading his books has meant to them. Mike loves seeing that excitement and being able to be a part of it.

For young people aspiring to be writers someday, Mike has one main piece of advice: read, read, read. "You don't have to read me," Mike says. "But just read. Read the best people... The greatest magic still is page one, chapter one of a book you want to read. Because once you open that book, it's like you're opening a door, not only to your imagination, but to my imagination as well." The best way to learn how to unlock your imagination, Mike feels, is to read.

After you read, read, read, the next step is to write, write, write. He says that the pressure of having to write a daily column prepared him well for the rigors of writing a book. Mike Lupica has spent years sitting down every day to write, and he continues to do so, even on days when he doesn't have a column due—not because he has to, but because he knows it will make him a better writer. Just like sports, he says, writing takes skill, practice, determination, and most importantly, the love of the job.

SELECTED BOOKS BY MIKE LUPICA

Travel Team (2004)

Heat (2006)

Miracle on 49th Street (2007)

Hot Hand (2007)

Two-Minute Drill (2007)

Safe at Home (2008)

Long Shot (2008)

Summer Ball (2008)

The Big Field (2008)

Million-Dollar Throw (2009)

Shoot-Out (2010)

The Batboy (2010)

Hero (2010)

The Underdogs (2011)

Game Changers (2012)

Game Changers: Play Makers (2013)

True Legend (2013)

Game Changers: Heavy Hitters (2014)

QB1 (2014)

GLOSSARY

autobiography—a story of a person's life written primarily by that person

bombardier—a person in a bomber aircraft who is responsible for aiming and releasing bombs

Civil Rights Movement—a social movement in the 1950s and 1960s that aimed to end discrimination against African Americans

columnist—a person who writes a column for a newspaper or magazine

cross-country—long-distance running

genre—a category of art, music, or literature in which the compositions share similarities in subject, form, or style

marathon—a 26.2-mile (42 km) race

novelist—a person who writes fiction books

Renaissance man—a person with many diverse talents or interests

sportsmanship—behaving in a gracious manner whether you win or lose a game

steroids—a type of drug prescribed by a doctor but sometimes used illegally to enhance performance; most professional sports ban the use of steroids

syndication—published simultaneously in many newspapers or magazines

teleplay—a script written for television

CHRONOLOGY

May 11, 1952: Born in Oneida, New York.

1962: Visits Baseball Hall of Fame in Cooperstown, New York, and decides he wants to have a career in sports.

1964: Moves to Nashua, New Hampshire, with his family.

1970: Graduates from Bishop Guertin High School and goes to Boston College. Begins writing stories for Boston College's newspaper, *The Heights*.

1974: Graduates from Boston College. Hired by *New York Post* to cover the Knicks.

1975: Lands job as youngest columnist ever hired by the *New York Daily News*.

1984: Publishes first book, *Reggie: The Autobiography of Reggie Jackson*, written with Reggie Jackson.

1986: Marries Taylor McKelvy in Bridgehampton, Long Island. Publishes *Dead Air*.

1987: Nominated for Edgar Allen Poe Award for Best First Mystery Novel for *Dead Air*.

1989: *Money, Power, Murder*, a TV movie based on the novel *Dead Air*, airs on CBS.

2003: Wins NFL's Jim Murray Award.

2004: Publishes *Too Far* as well as *Travel Team*, his first book for young readers.

2007: Launches Comeback Kids series.

2008: Publishes *Long Shot*, *Safe at Home*, *Summer Ball*, and *The Big Field*.

2011: Wins title of 2010 New York Sportswriter of the Year from the National Sportscasters and Sportswriters Association.

2012: Wins Damon Runyon Award for Journalism.

FURTHER INFORMATION

Books

Want to read the books that inspired Mike to be a writer? Check out these first books in each of Mike's favorite series for young readers:

Bee, Clair. *Touchdown Pass*. New York, NY: Grosset & Dunlap, 1948.

Blaine, John. *The Rocket's Shadow*. New York, NY: Grosset & Dunlap, 1947.

Dixon, Franklin W. *The Tower Treasure* (The Hardy Boys No. 1). New York, NY: Grosset & Dunlap, 1927.

Websites

Mike Lupica's Official Website
www.mikelupicabooks.com

Mike's website contains descriptions of many of his books for young readers, a brief biography, a link to his newspaper columns, and answers to some frequently asked questions.

Mike Lupica's Column in the *New York Daily News*
www.nydailynews.com/authors?author=Mike%20Lupica

Mike Lupica's column in the *New York Daily News* is the best place to stay up-to-date with his opinions on major sports news.

BIBLIOGRAPHY

ONLINE SOURCES

"About Mike Lupica." Penguin.com (USA). Retrieved February 23, 2014 from http://www.us.penguingroup.com/nf/Author/AuthorPage/0,,1000009423,00.html

Library of Congress. "Mike Lupica: 2012 National Book Festival." YouTube, May 9, 2013. Retrieved February 23, 2014 from http://www.youtube.com/watch?v=ifDOhTYnY-0

Lupica, Mike. "Mike Lupica Talks Sportsmanship in Young Athletes." Today Show, February 7, 2013. Retrieved February 23, 2014 from http://www.today.com/video/today/50730456

Mike Lupica blog. Retrieved February 23, 2014 from http://mikelupica.blogspot.com/

"Mike Lupica." Books 4 Boys. Retrieved February 23, 2014 from http://www.us.penguingroup.com/static/packages/us/yreaders/books4boys/author_mikelupica.php

"Mike Lupica." TeachingBooks.net. Retrieved February 23, 2014 from http://www.teachingbooks.net/tb.cgi?aid=2509&a=1

"Mike Lupica, the Daily News Sports Section's Leading Voice, Named New York Sportswriter of the Year." *Daily News*, January 10, 2011. Retrieved February 23, 2014 from http://www.nydailynews.com/sports/mike-lupica-daily-news-sports-section-leading-voice-named-new-york-sportswriter-year-article-1.149270

Shalhoup, Mike. "For Lupica, It All Started Here." *The Telegraph*, October 24, 1993. Retrieved February 23, 2014 from http://news.google.com/newspapers?nid=2209&dat=19931024&id=I5ZKAAAAIBAJ&sjid=DJQMAAAAIBAJ&pg=4838,5392050

Williams, Maya. "Mike Lupica Masters Two Trades." Scholastic.com. Retrieved February 23, 2014 from http://www.scholastic.com/teachers/article/mike-lupica-masters-two-trades

INDEX

ABOUT THE AUTHOR:

Cathleen Small started reading at the age of three and has never stopped. As a child, she spent countless hours reading and rereading her favorite books. These days, she edits and writes books, too, but reading is still her favorite thing to do. She particularly enjoys reading funny and magical books to her two young sons, Theo and Sam. Cathleen, her book-loving husband, their two boys, and their two pugs (who eat books more than read them) live outside of San Francisco, California.